The Lost Keys to Success
and Happiness

*The ordinary persons guide to
living an extraordinary life*

By Trenna Pennington

Copyright 2007 by Trenna Pennington
All rights reserved. No part of this book may
be used or reproduced in any manner
whatsoever without written permission,
except in the case of brief quotations
embodied in critical articles or reviews.
Published 2007
Updated 2018

ISBN: 9781521720219

If you believe it, you will achieve it!

A purpose in life is the only fortune
worth finding; and it is not to be found
in foreign lands, but in the heart.

If you cannot do great things yourself,
you can always do small things in
a great way.

You have within you the power to
transform your life…
You have the power to transform your
thoughts and dreams
into physical reality.

Greatness comes to those who develop a
burning desire to achieve high goals

To become an expert, it takes
practice… practice… practice.

Man's greatest power lies in
the power of prayer.

The Fifteen Keys:

The First Key: Passion – *The Physician* – A very knowledgeable man. He uses astrology to help him diagnose and cure people.

The Second Key: Confidence – *The Wife from Bath* – A housewife who is very authoritative and always wants to be first. She has had 5 husbands and likes to travel.

The Third Key: Abundance – *The Guildsman* – A skilled worker and good businessman.

The Fourth Key: Initiative – *The Franklin* – He is generous, wealthy and loves to entertain.

The Fifth Key: Imagination – *The Clerk* – A struggling student who spends all his money on books instead of food and clothes.

The Sixth Key: Enthusiasm – *The Man of Law* – He is wise, and his knowledge of the law is extensive.

The Seventh Key: Discipline – *The Prioress* – She is graceful, pretty, and a social climber. A charming fraud.

The Eighth Key: Excel – *The Yeoman* – An expert in military gear he is the servant to the Knight and Squire.

The Ninth Key: Character – *The Reeve* – A shrewd, dishonest but highly skilled carpenter.

The Tenth Key: Vision – *The Squire* – The knight's son is a knight in training; he is highly skilled in jousting and is the quintessential playboy.

The Eleventh Key: Focus – *The Shipman* - A master sailor but very ruthless.

The Twelfth Key: Teamwork–*The Merchant* – A businessman who always talks about business. A work-a-holic.

The Thirteenth Key: Perseverance – *The Plowman* – A hard worker with strong faith.

The Fourteenth Key: Tolerance – *The Knight* – A world renowned jouster, a warrior, a perfect nobleman.

The Fifteenth Key: Faith – *The Monk* – He visits the bars more than he visits the poor and he doesn't take his vows very seriously.

The Lost Keys to Success and Happiness

We're all on a quest for success and happiness. Defining success and happiness is a matter of personal choice. I feel success is getting up every time you fall and trying again. Happiness is looking forward to the future and making memories with my family and those close to me.

During my mediation time I was reflecting on my times of trials. I have been blessed with many trials to over come and learn from. What I have learned I have shared with others. I have also been blessed with a wonderful family and countless friends.

Everything around us is in a constant state of momentum. It all starts with an electron. Electrons are constantly moving. They revolve around their atom's nuclei at amazing speeds. Atoms form stars, trees, mice, elephants, humans, and even gold. The movement of these electrons causes vibrations. The human ear can detect 32,000 to 38,000 vibrations per minute, we call it sound. At 3,000,000 vibrations per second generates light and higher still are the vibrations that hold your thoughts.

Each of us receives and gives off vibrations. We can "feel" another person's stress, enthusiasm at a sports event, or tension in a room.

Embedded in n your thoughts, you hold an invisible source of energy, untapped power that only you have the key to unlock.

Many people have traveled to Canterbury with a desire for spiritual replenishment and rejuvenation. Fifteen lives were transformed by an encounter with a stranger. They left Canterbury not only renewed but inspired. Each one from a different walk of life and each one with a story tell.

The First Key

PASSION

I am an educated man. I was schooled in medicine, astrology, and physics. I came from humble beginnings as most men do, but during my stay in Canterbury, a wise man came to me and gave me a key. "There are fifteen keys and used together they will unlock your deepest dreams and greatest successes and make your desires a reality. The only stipulation is that you must pass on the key to those with whom you come in contact."

So, I am writing this to share with you, the first key to unlock your deepest dreams and greatest successes. I am only to share my key, as others are to share with you the remaining keys.

A burning desire, a defining purpose for your life, passion. It sounds simple, but it must be put into action.

Any passionate desire that is set in your mind and held there, with the determination to realize it creates a focus so strong that your subconscious mind affects your physical actions and you start moving towards achieving that desire.

2   The Lost Keys to Success

Once you know you defining purpose, it should be written out and placed where you will see it throughout the day.

The effect of this is to impress this purpose upon your subconscious mind so strongly that it acts as a blueprint. This blueprint will dominate your activities in life and lead you, toward the attainment of that purpose.   This suggestion, which you repeatedly make to yourself, is a form of self-hypnosis. Do not be apprehensive of it, for it was through the aid of this principle that I rose from my humble beginnings.   Be sure that your purpose is constructive and that when you attain it you will not bring hardship and misery to anyone.

Revitalizing your mind with your passion will attract you to people who will be able to help you. Is your desire far above your present circumstances in life? You owe it to yourself and to the community in which you live to set a high standard for yourself. All great leaders base their leadership upon a passionate pursuit of their purpose. People will follow a leader when they know that their leader is a person with a purpose and who has the courage to back up that purpose with action

If success depends upon power, and if power is an organized effort, the first step in the direction of organization is a defining purpose. Therefore, a defining purpose is essential.

Until you select a defining purpose in life your thoughts are scattered over so many subjects and in so many different directions that they do not lead to power, but to indecision and weakness.

With the aid of a small magnifying glass you can teach yourself a great lesson on the value of organized effort. Using such a glass you can focus the sun-rays on a definite spot so strongly that they will burn a hole through a plank. Remove the glass (which represents the definite purpose) and the same rays of sun may shine on that same plank for a million years without burning it.

Building alliances with others (an organized effort) who share the same desire/defining purpose but think differently or have different skills, removes all limitations on what you can accomplish.

Millions of people who concentrate on poverty and failure are getting both in over abundance. Are you passionate about your defining purpose or focusing on poverty and fear of failure?

No man ever achieved worth-while success who did not, at one time or another; find himself on the brink of failure.

Passion is the factor which determines what your defining purpose in life shall be. No one can select your passion for you, but once you have it, it occupies the spotlight of your mind until it is satisfied by transformation into reality.

What is the formula for transforming desire, defining purpose, dreams into reality? *Know what you want, when you want it, why you want it and HOW you intend to get it.*

Take this one last thought with you: Nature cannot be tricked or cheated. She will give up to you the object of your struggles only after you have paid her price, which is *continuous, unyielding, and persistent effort.*

The First Key: Passion

Worksheet:

1. Fix in your mind the exact amount of money you want.
I want $_____ by _____
                            (month/day/year)

2. Determine exactly what you intend to give in return for the money you desire. "You give before you get." What is your plan for acquiring the money?

_____

_____

_____

3. What are you going to sell?

_____

_____

4. How many are you going to sell?

_____

5. Read your written statement aloud, twice a day. See and feel and believe yourself already in possession of the money.

The Second Key

CONFIDENCE

As a child I was teased and taunted. I was the short, stubby girl with big glasses. I spent my life trying to be happy by buying expensive clothes and fancy hats. I had many husbands and made them all miserable because I was miserable. I feared criticism. That all changed while I was staying in Canterbury with friends. As I was walking in the gardens, a man approached me, and we got to talking. What he shared with me was the second key of fifteen. "The keys used together will unlock your deepest dreams and greatest successes, make your desires reality." He said, "The only stipulation is that you must pass on the key to those you come in contact with." Now, I am sharing with you the key that I was given and the one that changed my life forever.

You can do anything if you believe you can.

Fear destroys our self-confidence. Fear of failure, success, criticism, or defeat. If we allow fear to control us, success and happiness are impossible. "Fear is the

The Second Key: Confidence

dungeon of the mind into which we hide. Fear brings superstition, which is the dagger that assassinates the soul". The irony is that what we fear is what makes us strong. Defeat, failure, and criticism are great learning tools, if we accept them as such. Do you want to condemn yourself to poverty, misery and failure? No! You want to soar to heights of great achievement! You decide your fate solely by the thoughts you think.

If you demand success of yourself and reinforce this demand with consistent action, you are sure to win. Within you is the power to achieve whatever you want. The best way to use this power is to believe in yourself. Don't be afraid of mistakes, you learn what works and what doesn't. Push yourself to do your very best; it breeds self-control, strength of will, contentment and countless other virtues which benefit you the rest of your life.

Don't stop even when you struggle. Dream, plan and imagine the things you want to come to you. Our minds become filled with dominant thoughts and we attract forces, people and circumstances which harmonize with the nature of these thoughts.

Give more than you get in your relationships, your work and charity. Great leaders inspire others by suggestion and kindness rather than by force. Success and fulfillment are dependent on you. However, you need the co-operation of others to attain success of a far-reaching nature and to get that co-operation renew your mind with the positive attitude of self-confidence. If your backup this belief with dynamic, aggressive action, others will know that you believe in your self.

Confidence is contagious; it is compelling, persuasive and it attracts others. Any statement that you repeatedly make to yourself, or any desire that you deeply plant in your mind, will eventually seek expression through your physical, outward bodily effort. Where thought prevails, power may be found. You will find amazing things start to happen and your life will be transformed just as mine was. I have traveled through distant countries and learned many cultures and am respected by those whom I met along my life's journey. I am a confident woman.

The Second Key: Confidence

Confidence Formula

I know that I have the ability to achieve the object of my passionate purpose...

I demand of myself persistent, aggressive and consistent action towards my goals.

I realize that my dominate thoughts reproduce themselves in outward, bodily action and transform themselves into physical reality. Any desire or goal that I constantly hold in my mind becomes reality.

I have clearly mapped out and written down a description of my definite purpose in life and know the importance of aligning the material and spiritual aspects of my existence.

No wealth or position can last unless it is built upon truth and justice.

I refuse to engage in any transaction that does not benefit all involved.

I will inspire others to serve me because I will first serve them.

A negative attitude never brings success. Others will believe in me because I believe in them and myself.

I choose to live modesty and give generously of my time and finances.

It is through struggles and challenges that I will find opportunities.

The Third Key

ABUNDANCE

My biggest regret is that I spent all my money. My father died when I was 20 and I inherited the family business. I worked hard to make it profitable, and in the beginning my wife and I had little money, yet we had as much happiness in those days as I have ever had since. The strange thing is that the experience of those days did not teach me the value of money. After the birth of my first son I had the burning desire to make the business even more profitable. I worked day and night to achieve this goal. All the money, however, passed out of my pockets as easily as water flows through a pipe. The more I made the more I spent. Now I've lost it all. So, I decided to come on this journey to Canterbury to re-evaluate my situation for I am at a dire loss.

One afternoon I went to the market, the man beside me started up a conversation. What he shared with me was the third key of fifteen. "The keys used together will unlock your deepest dreams and greatest successes, make your desires reality." He said, "The only stipulation is that you must pass on the key to those you come in contact with."

The Third Key: Abundance

Now, I am sharing with you the key that I was given and the one that changed my life forever.

"The world is filled with an abundance of opportunity for the dreamer," he said. "Dream of abundance, fill your heart with desire to be wealthy. Every morning I pray *"Lord, bless me, enlarge my territory! Let your hand be with me and keep me from evil so that I may not cause pain."*

Money is not the root of evil it is a person's attitude which causes destruction or abundance

1. Stay away from debt. Debt is like a big black cloud hanging over you head, ready to drown you at a moments notice. Almost all people who live beyond their means think that life's fortune wheel will stop at the right time. They expect a huge windfall of money will end their indebtedness. The wheel usually stops at the wrong place and they end up more in debt then before. You are unable to create or carry out your purpose in life with heavy debt hanging over their head. If you are bound in debt you will become depressed and set limitations in your mind and cause your own failures.

2. Start saving money. No matter how old you are, if you can start saving a little money each day it will grow and grow. Having money saved is like having an umbrella for that rainy day.

3. Give. Giving a percentage of your income to a charity is going to bring sunshine into your life. Everyone can give. What you get in return is far more valuable then what you give.

4. Volunteer. Volunteering your time is like letting rays of sunshine warm your soul. Wherever you are in life there is always someone somewhere worse off then you.

5. Smile and let the sunshine of happiness into your soul. Smiles are contagious. Smiling is an exercise that forces your mind to accept happiness. Try to smile at least five times a day.

These habits build up your character attracting opportunities which result in abundance.

Every failure, every adversity, every heart-ache may be a blessing in disguise providing it changes the way you think. With health, faith, energy, optimism, and confidence you can carry out your passion and dreams until they are a

The Third Key: Abundance

reality. It is never too late in life to start, if you know that the only thing that can stop you is death."

I took this key to heart and have experienced abundance in all aspects of my life. One thing is certain: I have learned my lesson at last. I feel sure that opportunities will come my way and that my business will again be profitable. I live on 70% of my income. 10% for savings, 10% for giving and 10% for debts and when my debts are gone I will have 15% for savings and 15% for giving. Over the entrance to my business I placed the sign...

"WE TALK AND THINK ONLY OF ABUNDANCE HERE. IF YOU HAVE A TALE OF WOE PLEASE KEEP IT, AS WE DO NOT WANT IT."

If I allow myself to feel depressed over my past, or filled my mind with worries, I would not be capable of attaining abundance. Besides, I would be ungrateful to my Maker for having endowed me with wonderful health all my life. Is there any greater blessing?

Worksheet:

Start today. Put one dollar a day or empty your change into a jar or set up a savings account at the bank and put a portion of every deposit into that account.
Then every 6 months invest that savings. If you aren't sure where to invest it ask a financial consultant. Also keep a rainy-day fund available to provide for at least 2 months of your household expenses.

Give. Start today. Find a place where you can volunteer your time, pick something you find interesting. Try something new once in awhile. You have nothing to lose everything to gain. Give from your wallet as well. Research charities you are interested and then start giving.

Plan to start getting out of debt. A little at a time and it will soon be gone. Take any "Free money" like bonuses and tax returns and put that towards your debt.

SMILE ☺

The Fourth Key

IINIATIVE

I love life and all the luxuries it has to offer, especially food and wine. I used to wander from job to job before I was handed a large inheritance in my thirties, now I just freely spend my money as I wish, mostly at the pub with my friends. That was until I met a man at the courtyard in Canterbury. He shared with me the fourth key of fifteen. "The keys used together will unlock your deepest dreams and greatest successes, make your desires reality." He said, "The only stipulation is that you must pass on the key to those you come in contact with." Now, I am sharing with you the key that I was given. This key unlocked in me potential and courage I had never known. I may have had all the money I needed but I had never worked towards a goal or held a job for long or felt pride in anything I did.

"Initiative is the foundation that success is built upon." He started, "There are three different layers of initiative.

The top layer is comprised of the person who does the right thing without being told, the person who "does it NOW". This person creates opportunities for themselves when there seems to be no opportunities around.

The middle layer is the person who will do the right thing when necessity kicks them from behind. This person usually gets indifference instead of honors because they have excuses and hard luck stories to explain their lack of action.

The third and last layer is the person who will not do the right thing even when there is someone to go along to show him how to do it and goes along to show him how to do it and even stays to see that he does it right. This person is always out of a job and has no friends.

To become a person of initiative you must be aggressive and persistent in following the object of your passion until you acquire it, whether this requires one year or twenty years. The only way to get happiness is to give it. The same applies to initiative. The best way to develop initiative is to teach it to those around you. If we sow seeds of hatred, envy and discouragement in others, we start to develop these qualities in ourselves, but if we sow seeds of encouragement and initiative we develop those qualities. For some, money is a strong motivator but the person who works for money alone feels empty because there will never be enough money. No amount of

The Fourth Key: Initiative

money can take the place of the happiness, joy and pride that belongs to the person who digs a better ditch, sweeps a cleaner floor or cooks a better meal. Every one of us loves to create something that is better than the average. The only limitations we have are the ones we set in our mind.

Leaders take initiative and have a definite purpose in mind. They have confidence in themselves and their abilities to achieve their goals and the passion to pursue it. Leaders hold themselves to a strict account-ability. Leadership is a composite of several qualities. Among the most important I would list self-confidence, moral ascendancy, self-sacrifice, paternalism, fairness, initiative, decision, dignity, and courage. Lead by example. You must never fly off the handle. Remain calm and composed even in the most difficult situations. Live clean, so that you have enough brain power to see right and have the will to do it. Give praise and respect to those you encounter. Know your team, know your business, and know yourself.

Leaders and people with initiative must use co-operation with those they come in contact with. Co-operation is said to be the most important word in the English language. It is important in all types of relationships; in the relationship of man and wife, parents and children, leaders and team members. The principle of co-operation is so important that no leader can become powerful or last long if he does not understand and apply it in his leadership. Lack of co-operation has destroyed more businesses and families than have all other causes combined. If you want to succeed in doing something that helps the world you must practice these three words. SERVICE; SACRIFICE; SELF-CONTROL. The power of co-operation is so great that combined with harmonized effort from all the worlds' churches could stop wars, make schools, streets and neighborhoods safe. A united front of churches and businesses would end world hunger and homelessness.

 The first key was passion. Let it be here emphasized that your passion must be active and not passive. Passion will never be anything else but a mere wish unless you become a person of initiative and aggressively and persistently pursue that aim until it has been fulfilled.

The Fourth Key: Initiative

Lack of persistence achieves nothing; this fact cannot be repeated often enough.

The difference between persistence and lack of it is the same as the difference between wishing for a thing and positively determining to get it."

I went back to the Inn to reflect on what the man had said, and it occurred to me, that I could be a great leader. I wanted to know the joy of creating something better then the rest. I wanted people to respect me and help me pursue my passion. The man lit a spark in me I had never known and to this day I still practice the habit of initiative. I travel the world to teach others how to be great leaders in their lives.

Worksheet:

CHERISH your visions and your dreams as they are the children of your soul; the blueprints of your ultimate achievements.

Having chosen a definite purpose in my life, I now understand it to be my duty to transform this purpose into reality. Therefore, I will form the habit of taking some definite action each day that will carry me one step nearer the attainment of my definite purpose.

I know that procrastination is a deadly enemy of all who would become leaders in any undertaking, and I will eliminate this habit from my make-up by:

(a) Doing one definite thing each day, that ought to be done, without anyone telling me to do it.

(b) Looking around until I find at least one thing that I can do each day, that I have not been in the habit of doing, and that will be of value to others, without expectation of pay.

(c) Telling at least one other person, each day, of the value of practicing this habit.

I can see that the muscles of the body become strong in proportion to the extent to which they are used, therefore I understand that the

The Fourth Key: Initiative

habit of initiative also becomes fixed in proportion to the extent that it is practiced.

I realize that the place to begin developing the habit of initiative is in the small commonplace things that relate to my daily work, therefore I will go at my work each day as if I were doing it solely for the purpose of developing this necessary habit of initiative.

I understand that by practicing this habit of taking the initiative in connection with my daily work I will be not only developing that habit, but I will also be attracting the attention of those who will place greater value on my services because of this practice.

Try an experiment that will prove both interesting and profitable to you, pick out some person of your acquaintance whom you know to be a person who never does anything that he is not expected to do, and begin selling him your idea of initiative. Do not stop by merely discussing the subject once; keep it up every time you have a convenient opportunity. Approach the subject from a different angle each time. If you go at this experiment in a tactful and forceful manner you will soon observe a change in the person on whom you are trying the experiment.

And, you will observe something else of more importance still: You will observe a change in yourself!

You cannot talk initiative to others without developing a desire to practice it yourself

Attributes of a leader:
1. Courage and confidence.
2. Self control.
3. A keen sense of justice.
4. Definiteness of decision. If you waver in your resolve you send the message that you're not sure of yourself.
5. Definiteness of plans. The successful leader must plan his work and work his plan. A leader who moves by guesswork, without practical, definite plans, is comparable to a ship without a rudder.
6. The habit of doing more than paid for. Leaders work harder than followers.
7. A pleasing personality.
8. Sympathy and understanding.
9. Mastery of detail. (This can be learned)
10. Willingness to assume full responsibility. The leader must assume responsibility for the mistakes and shortcomings of his

followers. If he tries to shift this responsibility, he will not remain the leader.

If one of his followers makes a mistake, and is incompetent, the leader must consider that it is HE who failed. Choose your followers wisely.

11. Cooperation - leadership calls for power, and power calls for co-operation.

The Fifth Key

IMAGINATION

I guess you would call me studious. I spend much of my time and money on books of philosophy at the expense of my personal appearance and social life. My passion is to be a teacher. To be able to take knowledge and pass it on to others, I feel it is one of the greatest professions. As I wandered aimlessly around Canterbury, through the noisy markets and quiet gardens I happened upon a gentleman lying on his back in the middle of a field gazing up at the sky. Curious I asked him what he was doing. "Imagining" he said "just imagining what shapes the clouds make"

"Do you not read?" I exclaimed "do you not know that they are just millions of tiny droplets of water and ice and that they don't really make anything." "Son" he said "Imagination has been called the creative power of the soul. You will never know your passion; have self-confidence, initiative and leadership unless you first create these qualities in your imagination." He shared with me the fifth key of fifteen. "These keys used together will unlock your deepest dreams and greatest successes, make your

The Fifth Key: Imagination

desires a reality." He said, "The only stipulation is that you must pass on the key to those you come in contact with." Now, I am sharing with you the key that I was given. This key is used to unlock your imagination.

A bird develops from the germ that lies asleep in the egg, so will your material achievements grow out of the organized plans that you create in your imagination. First comes the thought; then, organization of that thought into ideas and plans; then transformation of those plans into reality. The beginning, as you will observe, is your imagination. Imagination is the only thing in the world over which you have absolute control. Others may deprive you of material wealth and cheat you in a thousand ways, but no man can deprive you of the control and use of your imagination. As a man of imagination, you must first create a definite purpose and then surround yourself with men who have the training and the vision necessary to transform that passion into reality.

If your imagination is the mirror of your soul, then you have a perfect right to stand before that mirror and see yourself as you wish to be. You have the right to see reflected in that magic mirror the mansion you intend to own, the factory you intend to manage, the bank of which you intend to be president, the station in life you intend to occupy, the thousands of students you have taught. Your imagination belongs to you! Use it! The more you use it the more efficiently it will serve you.

The fact that the greatest and most profitable thing you can do with your imagination is the act of rearranging old ideas in new combinations. If you properly use your imagination it will help you convert your failures and mistakes into assets of priceless value; it will lead you to the discovery of a truth known only to those who use their imagination; namely, that the greatest reverses and misfortunes of life often open the door to golden opportunities. If you feel that your own imagination is inadequate you should form an alliance with someone whose imagination is sufficiently developed to supply your deficiency. When trying to secure a sale or a request remember that when men won't grant you your request for your own benefit they will grant a request for the benefit of a third party. For example, if you are requesting books for your

The Fifth Key: Imagination

students offer the statement "not my sake, or for the school but for the children."

If the winds of fortune are temporarily blowing against you, remember that you can harness them and make them carry you toward your definite purpose, using your imagination. A kite rises against the wind - not with it!

The beginning is simple. It starts with an idea, which anyone might have developed, but you add determination, passion, the desire to attain the goal, and persistent effort. It is no ordinary desire that survives disappointment, discouragement, temporary defeat, criticism, and the constant reminding of "waste of time." It is a burning desire, an obsession!

Ideas are like that. First you give life, action and guidance to them, and then they take on power of their own and sweep aside all opposition.

Worksheet:

Imagination is the workshop where plans are created, and ideas flow freely. Take 10 minutes a day to close your eyes, shut the world out and dream, create and plan. Use your imagination to create new things out of existing ideas, or to inspire you to create new ideas. Ask questions "what if", "what would happen?", "How can I make it better, faster, stronger?" Your imagination only becomes stronger as you use it.

Write out your ideas: Brainstorm with others:

_____
_____
_____
_____
_____
_____
_____
_____
_____
_____
_____
_____
_____

The Sixth Key

ENTHUSIASM

While I was staying in Canterbury, I needed to have a message delivered to a judge in London. A man was on trial for his life and I had found some information that could set him free. It was imperative that this message reached the judge quickly. My problem was that I didn't know where the judge's primary residence was, and I only had a day to find him. I mentioned my predicament to a colleague, who suggested that I hire Harry. Harry took the letter, delivered it to London and was back within the day. My point is this; I gave the letter to Harry to be delivered to the judge. Harry took the letter and delivered it without asking a single question. Such as "where does the judge live? Will he be home? How long do I have? Is it very important? Truly outstanding. Many people could learn from Harry. Harry is loyal, acts promptly, concentrates on the task, and gets the job done.

I was making my way back to the inn when an older man approached me. He said that he had been following my career and was impressed. He also said that I was missing something. He then shared with me a key.

This was the sixth of fifteen- Enthusiasm. "The keys used together will unlock your deepest dreams and greatest successes, make your desires reality the only stipulation is that you must pass on the key to those you come in contact with."

Enthusiasm is a state of mind that inspires and arouses one to put action toward the task at hand. It is contagious, and affects not only the enthusiast, but all of those he encounters. The greatest leaders are those who know how to inspire enthusiasm in their followers.

Happiness, the object of all human effort, is a state of mind that can be maintained only through the hope of future achievement. Happiness always lies in the future and never in the past. The happy person is the one who dreams of heights of achievement that are yet unattained. The home you intend to own, the money you intend to make, the trip you intend to take when you can afford it, these are the things that produce happiness. These are the things which help you become enthusiastic, no matter what your present situation in life may be. You may be a long way from realizing your defining purpose, but if you kindle the fire of enthusiasm in your heart, and keep it burning. The obstacles that now stand in your way will melt away as if by force of magic. You will find yourself in possession of power that you never knew existed.

The three mediums through which enthusiasm operates are **what you say, what you do and what you think!** When you are enthusiastic over the goods you are selling or the services you are offering, or the speech you are delivering, your state of mind becomes obvious to all who hear you, by the tone of your voice. What you say is important but not as nearly as important as how you say it and by what you do. Your actions count more than your words. If your thoughts, actions, and words harmonize, you are bound to influence those with whom you come in contact.

Suggestion is one of the most subtle and powerful principles of psychology. You are making use of it in all that you do, say, and think. You need to understand the difference between negative and positive suggestions. You may be using them in such a way that it is bringing you defeat instead of success

It is not so much what you say as it is the TONE and WAY you say it that makes a lasting impression.

Follow the passion from your heart. You can not afford to try to deceive anyone, about anything, but most importantly I know that you cannot afford to deceive yourself. To do so would destroy you. It is only when enthusiasm burns in your heart it impresses others and it is only when you speak from a heart that is bursting with belief that you can move your audience to accept that message.
All anyone really requires to be successful is a sound mind, a healthy body and a genuine desire to be of as much service as possible to as many people as possible.

Success attracts success! Therefore, if you wish to attract success make sure that you look the part of success, whether you're calling is that of day laborer or merchant prince."

I took the advice of the man and I used Harry as my inspiration. I gave my career purpose to serve as many as I could, and I did it with enthusiasm. My life feels more fulfilled and I am happy as well as very successful.

The Sixth Key: Enthusiasm

Worksheet:

Remember first Impressions really do count. Dress for success.

To develop enthusiasm first write out your ultimate dream in life, and then write out a plan in which you intend to transform this dream into reality.
What is your dream?

_____
_____
_____
_____
_____
_____
_____
_____
_____
_____
_____
_____

Read over the description of your ultimate dream each night, just before bed, and as you read, see yourself in full possession of the object of your dream. Do this with full faith in your ability to transform your ultimate dream into reality. Read it out loud, emphasizing every word. Repeat this reading until the small still voice within you tells you that your purpose will be realized. Sometimes you will feel the effects of this voice from within the first time you read your ultimate dream; while at other times, you may have to read it a dozen or fifty times before the assurance comes, but do not stop until you feel it.

To become successful, you must be a person of action. Merely to "know" is not enough. It is necessary both to know and do.

One of the most valuable lessons any man can learn is the art of using the knowledge and experience of others

Enthusiasm is the mainspring of the mind which urges one to put knowledge into action.

The Seventh Key
DISIPLINE

Whether or not I was born with the proverbial silver spoon in my mouth, I can't say. My parents were well off. When I was seven, my father lost all his money and we had to move. We all faced a new life in a strange country. My father had to try and make a "come back" at the age of fifty in a different land. I had the handicap of not knowing a single word of the native language. I was sent to school to learn, but the teachers were impatient, and the other children were cruel. My father struggled to find work. My mother, who was used to having servants wait on her hand and foot, had to learn how to cook and clean. Everyday after school, my sister and I did all the chores to help mother. Mother detested the life we were living, but my sister and I remained positive, knowing that we needed to work hard to have a better life. Every Saturday when other children would play, my sister and I were cleaning the neighbors' houses to earn extra money for food.

I worked at many different jobs throughout the years to get where I am today. Those around me may think I am rich and shallow, but I have experienced poverty and cherished its lessons. I can empathize with the person going through it, but I would not like to go back.

I was in the market in Canterbury, shopping for some fruit for lunch when I met this man. We started discussing the fine, fresh produce the season had brought. We somehow got on the topic of success. He said that he wanted to share with me one of the keys to success. He then shared with me the seventh key of fifteen. "The keys used together will unlock your deepest dreams and greatest successes, make your desires reality." He said "The only stipulation is that you must pass on the key to those with whom you encounter.

A person must live a balanced life. Enthusiasm and discipline must be equal. Enthusiasm is the quality that arouses, you to act and discipline directs your actions in a positive manner. Be disciplined in every day tasks, such as closing your ears to gossip. Personally, I have developed the habit of "closing" my ears against idle talk that would make me resentful. Life is too short and there is too much constructive work to be done to justify us in "striking back" at everyone who says things that we don't like.

The Seventh Key: Disipline

A person that is disciplined will not permit himself to be influenced by the cynic or the pessimist; nor will he permit another person to do his thinking for him.

A person that is disciplined will stimulate his imagination and his enthusiasm until they have produced action, but he will then control that action and not permit it to control him.

A person that is disciplined will never, under any circumstances, slander another person or seek revenge for any cause whatsoever.

A person that is disciplined will not hate those who do not agree with him; instead, he will endeavor to understand the reason for their disagreement, and profit by it.

On the other hand, lack of discipline causes more grief than all other forms combined; it is the habit of forming opinions before studying the facts.

Make exercise a part of your daily routine. A healthy body is as important as a healthy mind. Save money instead of spending it. That little savings account will allow you to take advantage of many opportunities come your way. The size of the account is not as important as the fact that you have established the savings habit.

This habit marks you as a person who exercises an important form of self-control and discipline.

Control your words and actions. Words are sharper then a sword and most of all listen more and talk less. You are the only one who controls your thoughts. The power is yours for the taking. Dominate your thoughts with your passion and goals and they will become a reality. Start by saying to yourself, YES, it CAN be done. You are the product of at least a million years of evolutionary change. For countless generations preceding you Nature has been tempering and refining the materials that have gone into your make-up. Step by step, she has removed from the generations that have preceded you the animal instincts and base passions until she has produced, in you, the finest specimen of animal that lives. She has endowed you, through this slow evolutionary process, with reason and poise and "balance" enough to enable you to control and do with yourself whatever you will.

No other animal has ever been endowed with such self-control as you possess. You have been endowed with the power to use the most highly organized form of energy known to man, that of thought. It is probable that thought is the closest connecting link there is between the material, physical things of this world and the world of Divinity.

You have not only the power to think but, what is a thousand times more important still, you have the power to control your thoughts and direct them to do your bidding! You are searching for the magic key that will unlock the door to the source of power; and yet you have the key in your own hands, and you may make use of it the moment you learn to control your thoughts. Place in your own mind, through the principle of Auto-suggestion, the positive, constructive thoughts which harmonize with your passion and goals in life, and that mind will transform those thoughts into physical reality and hand them back to you, as a finished product. This is thought-control!
When you deliberately choose the thoughts, which dominate your mind and firmly refuse admittance to outside suggestion, you are exercising discipline in its highest and most efficient form. Man is the only living animal that can do this.

How does one go about controlling one's thoughts when in a state of intense anger? In the same way that you would change your manner and the tone of your voice if you were in a heated argument with a member of your family and a stranger was walking up the path towards you. You would control yourself because you would desire to do so." When you find it necessary to cover up your real feelings and change the expression on your face quickly, you know how easily it can be done, and you also know that it can be done because you want to do it! In an instant you can change your thoughts. Behind all achievement, behind all discipline, behind all thought control, is that magic something called DESIRE! In fact, you are limited only by the depth of your desires! When your desires are strong enough you will appear to possess superhuman powers to achieve. And when you reach your goals and are successful remember that someone, somewhere, sometime believed in you, and gave you an idea to start you in the right direction. You are indebted to life until you help someone less fortunate than you."

I realized in that moment that I had been inspired by a neighbor I had cleaned for. She helped me believe in myself when others

The Seventh Key: Disipline   41

around me where falling apart. I decided I needed to fulfill my purpose and help other women like me who needed to be inspired. I started a women's' club where I could mentor others and help them find success and happiness.

Worksheet:

Don't say "I can't do it" Plant in your mind the seed of a desire that is constructive and the code of your ethics.

My Code of Ethics
"I wish to be of service to the people around me as I journey through life.
I will train myself to never under any circumstances to find fault with any person as I know that they are sincerely trying to do their best.
I respect my country, my profession and myself. I am honest and fair in my dealings with others and expect the same in return.
I know that success lies within me and I have the power to change my circumstances and my thoughts. I expect obstacles to be overcome and I will persevere.
I will avoid procrastination by doing all the tasks that need to be done today, today.
I will enjoy life; I will not take anything for granted. I am thankful for my health, my family, my friends and difficulties.
I will listen more and talk less.
I will save more and spend less."

The Eighth Key

EXCEL

My employer had sent me into town on an errand; I was so focused on getting my task down that a light tap on my shoulder startled me. I turned around to stand face to face with a man I hadn't seen in town before. His clothes were simple enough, he had graying hair, and his moustache and beard were neatly trimmed. His face was wrinkled by time, yet he seemed kind and had an aura of wisdom about him. "I'm sorry I startled you." He said. "I have noticed your loyalty and dedication to your employer. I think it is quite commendable." "Thank you, sir, but my employer is quite demanding, and I am thinking of quitting." I replied.

"Son" he said "Let me share with you a key, this key is the eighth of fifteen and used together the keys will unlock your deepest dreams and greatest successes. They will turn your desires into reality. The only stipulation is that you must pass on the key to those you encounter.

Instead of quitting because there are obstacles to master and difficulties to overcome, just face the facts… life is just one long series of mastering obstacles and problems. We grow stronger the more resistance we have. A great man is always willing to learn new things about himself. When you are pushed, tormented, and defeated you have a chance to sharpen your wits and shine in adversity. Experience is irreplaceable, whether it is positive or negative. Perhaps you are training for a race or you want to lose weight, or you want to be healthier, the best way to achieve a goal is to set a high standard, set a goal that seems unreachable. Each day you train press yourself a little bit farther than the day before. If you walked a mile yesterday walk ½ mile more today. Under the resistance your body will become stronger and your mind will be focused and driven on attaining that unreachable goal. This is to Excel in a subject, to go the extra mile. You can do more then is expected of you.

    Make it part of your daily routine to surpass all previous records in every aspect of your life. In business you will make yourself invaluable to your employer and he will treat you as such. If you give better service, you will find that the world is willing to pay you according to your service level."

The Eighth Key: Excel

Maybe I had not been doing my best. I decided to give my job another try. This time I would go the extra mile. I will train others in my job and help them succeed. By helping them succeed I can help myself succeed.

Worksheet:

During the next six months do a random act of kindness to at least one person every day, something that you will not expect to be paid. Go into this experiment with the faith that you will enter the achievement of enduring success.

You can do these acts personally to a specific person, or group of people. You can stay longer after work, or you can give your services to strangers who you will never see again. You must carry out this experiment with a heart of willingness to benefit others. Carried out with a positive attitude this experiment will allow you to personally experience the key of Excel. By helping others, you are helping yourself succeed, by using the habit of performing more service and better service than which you are paid, you are taking advantage of the law of increasing returns.

Go back and review the keys of Initiative and Enthusiasm, they will become clearer to you.

One thing is clear by taking the initiative, following it with aggressive action and going the extra mile you will be a changed person no matter whom you are or where you live.

The Eighth Key: Excel

Take action! Do 5 things a day that will bring you closer to achieving your dream. DO IT NOW! I DARE YOU!

5 Things I will do today: Date:

1. _____
2. _____
3. _____
4. _____
5. _____

5 Things I will do today: Date:

1. _____
2. _____
3. _____
4. _____
5. _____

5 Things I will do today: Date

1. _____
2. _____
3. _____
4. _____
5. _____

5 Things I will do today: Date

1. _____
2. _____
3. _____
4. _____
5. _____

5 Things I will do today: Date

1. _____
2. _____
3. _____
4. _____
5. _____

5 Things I will do today: Date

1. _____
2. _____
3. _____
4. _____
5. _____

5 Things I will do today: Date

1. _____
2. _____
3. _____
4. _____
5. _____

The Ninth Key

CHARACTER

Win at all costs, whatever it takes…flattery, double taxing, and cheating, if it gets me lots of money I'll do it. As a carpenter, a highly skilled one I might add, I can create a masterpiece in a few days and triple my costs. I am meeting with one of the wealthiest men in the country. He has asked me to make some custom furniture for his study. The road leading up to the estate was lined with cherry blossoms. The house itself wasn't what you call stately, but it was very large. I was surprised to see an older man answer the door, I expected the butler. The inside of the house was nicely decorated, and the smell of apple pie drifted into the sun room where we were drinking tea.

"Son, I've asked around and you are a very skilled carpenter, yet people tell me they've been cheated out of money. I want to share with you a key, this key is the ninth of fifteen and used together the keys will unlock your deepest dreams and greatest successes. They will turn your desires into reality. The only stipulation is that you must pass on the key to those you encounter." He said "There is a great power of attraction behind the person who has a positive character. This power expresses itself through the invisible as well as the visible. You see it in their eyes, in their smile, even in the warmth of their hand shake. The moment you come within speaking distance of a positive person you can feel the positive energy they give off.

Every "shady" transaction that you engage in, every negative thought you think destroys a little piece of you. The more pieces you destroy the less character you have left.

Building character takes time but it is well worth it in the long run. Build your character and reputation by studying other people. Find out something about them, that you sincerely admire. Listen to others to find out their interests and good qualities and talk with them. Talk to them about their interests and not your agenda. When you speak, speak with conviction. When you shake hands do it so that you express warmth and enthusiasm.

Aspire to inspire others. Aspiration is greater than realization, because it keeps us eternally climbing upwards towards some unattainable goal. The only limitations are the ones you set in your mind."

The Nineth Key: Character

Take your joy of work and learn to love people and serve them. Your life will be changed."

I went away that day with more than a furniture order; I walked away with a new attitude and aspirations for a greater life. My reputation was on the line and I was ready to prove myself.

Worksheet:

Character building blocks:

First: Find a person or persons whose character is made up of the qualities you admire and which you wish to build into your own character.
Person/People I admire

_____
_____
_____
_____
_____
_____
_____
_____

Write out a clear statement of the qualities of each person you wish to develop in yourself.

_____
_____
_____
_____

The Nineth Key: Character

Create in your imagination, a council table, gather your characters around it each night and say out loud to yourself that you are now developing the qualities which you admire in your characters. Close your eyes as you see the figures seated with you around that table.

Second: Control your thoughts and keep your mind on the positive. Let your dominant thoughts be a picture of the person you intend to be. At least 10 times a day, when you have a few minutes to yourself, shut your eyes and direct your thoughts to the figures at your imaginary council table and feel with a faith that knows no limitations that you are growing to resemble in character those figures.

Third: Find a good quality in at least one person a day and praise that person. It must be sincere and with enthusiasm. Always look for and find the good qualities in others. This habit will modify your entire personality you will soon reflect those same qualities.

The Tenth Key

VISION

Lying in bed, I felt the warmth of the sun on my cheek. I opened my eyes and I was in my room at the Inn. What day was it? How long had I been asleep? Days? Weeks? It all seemed like a dream, yet I had the scars all over me to prove it was very real.

I remember traveling to Canterbury for a tournament. I was just outside of town when my horse was spooked and headed towards the woods. I was lost and just wandered in circles for what seemed to be hours, when I was suddenly struck from behind. Five men had beaten me, taken my horse and left me for dead. Luckily a man was passing through and found me and took me to his home. I can still smell the apple pie his wife made; it was the best I had ever tasted.

While I was recovering the man and I had many long discussions. The most important one was when he gave me a key. "Son" he said." Believe you will get better. Have faith that you will make a full recovery. Keep saying to yourself every day in everyway I'm getting better and better. I want to share with you a key. This is the tenth of fifteen keys and used together they

The Tenth Key: Vision

will unlock your deepest dreams and greatest successes. They will turn your desires into reality. The only stipulation is that you must pass on the key to those you encounter.

Your sub-conscious is the link between the conscious thinking mind and infinite intelligence. This allows you to tap into a force greater than yourself. The main characteristics of your sub-conscious is that it records the instructions you send it through the thoughts you think whether positive or negative and invokes the help of infinite intelligence to transform those thoughts into physical form. Picture a goal in your mind then fix your conscious mind on that goal with such intensity that it communicates with your sub-conscious mind and registers that goal. Have full faith and confidence that opportunities will come, and doors will open to you at the proper time. Have patience and keep pursuing that dream.

You can change your world. Stop blaming others for your failures. Take responsibility for your life. You were born to be a champion; to be the best of the best. Everyone is born with the talent needed to achieve great things. In the history of the world there has never been anyone exactly

like you... Remember that real wealth can be measured not by what you have but what you are. I asked the man how he acquired his wealth. He replied.
"I found happiness by helping others find it
I found health by eating foods my body needs
I hate no man, envy no man, but love and respect all mankind
I love what I do so I seldom grow weary
I pray daily for more wisdom to recognize, embrace and enjoy the abundance I already possess
I am free from greed and only have what I need
I give of my time and money to charitable causes
I am thankful for all I have been blessed with and enjoy sharing it with those around me."

It all fell into place...The man and his wife had nurtured me back to health both physically and spiritually. I pictured them in my mind and then my goals; my biggest goal was to be world champion. I now had the ability to mentally and physically prepare for my tournaments and achieve my goal.

The Tenth Key: Vision

Worksheet:

Work smarter not harder. Separate the facts from most important to least important. Do not accept "I see in the papers" and "they say" as fact. Do your own research to find the true facts.

When you are in bed about to go to sleep that is the best time to turn on your sub conscious. Say to yourself "I want to wake up at____o'clock tomorrow." Repeat it several times and your sub conscious will wake you up in the morning at ____o'clock.
You must command it in no uncertain terms. Now each night plant your sub conscious with orders of the things in life you want to accomplish.

You first created the object towards which you are striving through your imagination. Then you wrote down a definite statement of your life's purpose. By daily reading that statement, it has been taken up in the conscious mind and handed over to the sub conscious mind, which then directs all the energies of your body, to transform that desire into reality.

Replace old bad habits with new good habits.

1. Start with one at a time, put enthusiasm into it, feel what you think. Make the path clear so that it will be easy to follow it next time.

2. Focus on the new path, forget about the old paths.

3. Practice your new habits as much as possible.

4. Resist the temptation to go back to the old habits. The first few times it will be hard but as you persist it will get easier.

5. Select your goal and move full steam ahead, without fear and doubt.

Create a good environment. Surround yourself with people you admire and who support you. People whose mental attitude inspires you with enthusiasm, confidence, determination and ambition.
Listen to upbeat tempo music when you are feeling down. Think positively!
Carefully select books that are in tune with your goals and inspire and educate you.

The Tenth Key: Vision

Dress for success. Look good, feel great.

Improve your memory.
First: When you want to recall a date or name. Repeat it several times to imprint it in your mind. Focus on it.

Second: Associate the thing you want to remember with another object, name or place that is already familiar to you. For example, the name of your close friend or a word that rhymes with it.

My Pledge: (Fill in the blanks)
I am going to become a
_____
Because this will enable me to give the world a service that is needed and because it will yield me a financial return that will provide me with the necessary material things in life.
I will concentrate my mind on this desire for ten minutes daily. Just before bed at night and just after waking in the morning, for planning how to transform it into reality.
I know that I can become a_____
Therefore, I will permit nothing to interfere with my doing so.

The Eleventh Key

FOCUS

I had been in Canterbury for almost six months and was anxious to get back to sea. My crew was gathering supplies in town, and as I was sitting on the dock waiting for them to return, an elderly gentleman approached me and asked where we were sailing to next. I told him that we were explorers and treasure hunters and never know where we would end up next. As we spoke, he seemed genuinely excited about some of our "adventures". He asked if I would entertain the idea of him accompanying us on this next voyage. He wanted some excitement in his life, he said. Just as I was about to say no, he said that he would pay handsomely. I had a spot left on board since I put the former deck hand off the ship - the lad kept getting sea sick. We set out shortly after dawn the next day. The conditions were perfect until we were about 40 miles out. A storm suddenly appeared. Heavy rain, gale winds, and huge swells enveloped my ship. The boom of the thunder was deafening, and then the unthinkable happened – lightning had struck the ship, and she splintered into dozens of pieces. I must have blacked out when I awoke I had a

The Eleventh Key: Focus

throbbing headache and was on a life boat with the older man. All my gold, all the treasures I had acquired gone! "I've lost everything!" I yelled to the sea.

"No, son you haven't. I'm here to give you the magic key you have been searching for", the old man said. I brandished my gun and told him to hand it over. No one was going to get away with the key to a treasure, not when I had just lost everything.

"Son", he said again, "the key is not a material possession. It is in your mind, you've had it the whole time. Focusing on evil pursuits has been your downfall, but this key I am willing to share with you will bring you only good things. This key is the eleventh of fifteen and used together the keys will unlock your deepest dreams and greatest successes. Your desires will become reality. I attach only one stipulation - you must pass on the key to those you meet. The magic key will unlock the door to greater riches then you've ever seen. Failure turns into success, misery into happiness.

Focus means the ability through habit and practice to keep your mind on one subject until you are familiar with that subject and mastered it. The ability to control your attention and focus on one problem until you have solved it. Ambition and desire make focus successful. If your desire is strong enough and you use the magic key, you will attain it. Great men and women believe that the power of prayer operates using focus on attaining a deeply seated desire. Everything we create is first created in our imagination through desire and then brought into reality through focus.

Close your eyes and focus on where you see yourself in one year, what are you doing, where are you living, are you sitting on top of that pot of gold? Do you own a huge shipping company? Paint this picture clearly in your mind. Now do it for 5 years from now, then 10. Focus on these desires and see what happens. Use this key with the gifts you've been given to benefit your community, and in return you'll experience endless joy and success. Use your past mistakes and failures as learning tools and make the next 5 or 10 years a story of success. Make an honorable name for yourself and do the world a great service through your ambition, desire, and focus. If you believe it, you can achieve it!"

We were rescued finally. I was unhappy with the old fool's "pep talk", and barely spoke to him after we were picked up. However, over the weeks that followed, his words resonated through my mind and my spirit. I hold the magic key. My new journey begins, and I know where I am going because it exists in my mind.

Worksheet

Write out a short, clear statement of that which you intend to accomplish in the next year.

Financial: _____
_____

Career: _____
_____

Community Service: _____
_____

Family/friends: _____
_____

Fitness: _____
_____

Personal – learning, spiritual etc. _____
_____

The Eleventh Key: Focus

Places I want to visit.

_____

_____

Next 5 years...
Financial: _____

_____

Career: _____

_____

Community Service: _____

_____

Family/friends: _____

_____

Fitness: _____

_____

Personal – learning, spiritual etc. ____

_____

Places I want to visit. _____
_____
_____
_____

Next 10 years…
Financial: _____
_____

Career: _____
_____

Community Service: _____
_____

Family/friends: _____
_____

Fitness: _____
_____

Personal – learning, spiritual etc. ____
_____

The Eleventh Key: Focus

Places I want to visit. _____
_____
_____

Top ten things to do before I die…

1. _____
2. _____
3. _____
4. _____
5. _____
6. _____
7. _____
8. _____
9. _____
10. _____

Re-read your statements throughout the day You will begin to observe things that pertain to your statement even new opportunities will arise.

With your life's purpose planted in your subconscious hold in your heart the faith and belief in the realization of that purpose.
Picture yourself in possession of that object or achieved that goal.

Act the way you would act if you already held it. Do not doubt, just believe.

Remove the word impossible from your vocabulary. You can do anything you can imagine and believe that you can do it

Remember no failure is forever, it is a temporary defeat, and it is just a stepping stool to lift you higher.

The Twelfth Key

TEAMWORK

My London stores are doing extremely well this year. Sales have surpassed last years by almost 50%. So, I went to Canterbury with some friends to purchase some fine fabric. It was also a good opportunity to escape from my family for a while. The merchants in Canterbury were very co-operative and I made some great purchases. I bid farewell to the last merchant and walk down to the town square. I was not paying attention to where I was going and literally walked right into a man and dropped my fabrics all over the ground. I apologized, and he helped me pick up my things. "These are beautiful fabrics, they should fetch a good price in London", the gentleman said, and I agreed.

We decided to have lunch, and he seemed genuinely interested in my business. As we dined, the conversation steered to the subject of relationships. Business, marriage, friends, – all kinds of relationships. My business relationships were good; I belonged to a powerful merchant association and had many other business acquaintances. My marriage however was quite another matter. I was miserable, and I made sure that I made my wife miserable. He listened intently and had a look of compassion on his face as he spoke to me like I was his own child. "Son, I'm going to share with you a key. This key is the twelfth of fifteen, and together the keys will unlock your deepest dreams and greatest successes. Your desires will become reality. My only stipulation is that you must pass the key on to others with whom you come in contact.

"Relationships are vital to all aspects of life. Relationships require the co-operation of each person coming together for attaining a certain goal. In business, you organize your company with great talent and allow each person to do their job to the best of their ability and talents. You create a team environment, you have salespeople who sell, buyers who are experts in trading, and you leave the finances to those who manage them best. When you balance your business, giving each person a job that they enjoy and excel in, you create a pleasant and productive working environment. Music also helps to create a pleasant and productive environment. Music with a faster tempo stimulates people to a faster work pace.

The Twelfth Key: Teamwork

Background music played at a slower tempo helps to relieve stress.

People who work toward a unified purpose develop a super-power. Sports teams win consistently if the players are in harmony with each other. Business owners who work with a team reach higher financial goals. Husbands and wives, who live together in harmony working as a team, raise families, accumulate wealth, and fortune. Working at relationships makes them stronger. Balance your work with your family. Having dinner together is an easy way to have more time with your family. Relationships need constant attention and care to grow, put your heart and soul into each one and it will grow and prosper and so will you.

Take action to accomplish your goals and build solid relationships. Your body is made up of billions of cells influenced by your mind. If your **mind** is inactive your body will become inactive and lazy. Stimulate your body by stimulating your mind. Read a book or plan something you are enthusiastic about. Your body won't feel tired.

Keep a positive frame of mind. LAUGH, LAUGH, and LAUGH some more. After an unpleasant day or event, I go to a place where I won't disturb anyone, and I have a good laugh, even a forced one. After five minutes I feel freed from negative emotion. "

We took leave of each other and his sincere, yet no holds barred way of speaking captivated me and warmed my heart. Self examination proves to be painful, but I knew that I spent so much time growing my business that I neglected my wife and family. I need to make things right with them; I need a balanced schedule that includes exercise and family time. I also need to laugh and have a more positive attitude. Spending time with my family is sure to change my life and theirs – hopefully for the better. HA HA. I can't wait to get home….

Wow, I haven't said that in a long time! HAHA!

The Twelfth Key: Teamwork

Worksheet:

Any teams working together towards the same goal are unstoppable.

Work on yourself. Think of the things that you need to change and one by one make a new, good habit to replace the old, bad habit.

Motivate yourself by having hope and taking action in your life.

Motivate others by having faith in them.

Take time to spend with your family and friends. Appreciate them and thank them.

Listen to those who are speaking to you and respond by using their words in your sentence.

Smile.

Laugh: 5 minutes everyday, a good hearty laugh.

Sing. Sing along with the songs. You know you want to. It'll lift your spirit!

Start each day right. Get into action.
For example:
1. Drink a cup of hot water with lemon first thing in the morning before breakfast.
2. Take a hot shower followed by a cold shower to awaken your senses.
3. Drink at least 8 glasses of water a day.
4. Exercise daily, start out by walking around the neighborhood.
5. Eat healthy. Don't overeat. Choose breads with whole wheat or bran they are better for you than white bread. Have fruits and vegetables at every meal.

Surround yourself with great people.

Analyze yourself and determine what your best abilities are. Are you a promoter? Do you enjoy going out and getting sales or do you enjoy sitting behind the books? Both are valuable to a company.

Take action:
1. Start each day by doing the tasks you dislike the most
2. Place a memo at work and home.

"Don't tell them what you can do, show them!"

The Twelfth Key: Teamwork

Set your goals, set them high, set a deadline, and take action:

_____

_____

_____

_____

_____

_____

_____

_____

_____

_____

_____

_____

_____

_____

_____

_____

_____

_____

_____

The Thirteenth Key

PERSEVERANCE

I have lost and gained many fortunes. Each one gave me a valuable life lesson, but the most valuable lesson I learned was from an old man I had met in Canterbury.

It was many years ago, but I remember it clearly. It was noon; I was sitting at my usual table, in my usual pub, eating my usual lunch drinking my usual beer, planning my revenge on three former business associates. Only six months earlier I had the perfect life. Money, power, respect, a loving family and a place to call home. Within moments it was all taken from me. I was arrested and send to jail, my business gone, and all my money even my family left. I spent the next five months pleading my innocence from my dark, cold cell. No one would listen. I went on trial and my lawyer and friend declared that the charges were false and that I had been framed by three business associates. I was released every day since then I have been coming to this pub and plotting my revenge on them. Then last week an older man sat down, and we started talking, I told him how filled with rage I was and that the only thing keeping me going was the obsession with revenge I had.

The Thirteenth Key: Perverance

"Son, I understand your anger and pain. "I too was arrested under false charges. It was a humiliating experience, but I realized that I needed to forgive my enemies for time would take care of them. Which it did, within a year they were both in jail for life for other offenses. Son, I'm going to share with you a key, this key is the thirteenth of fifteen and used together the keys will unlock your deepest dreams and greatest successes. They will turn your desires into reality. The only stipulation is that you must pass on the key to those with whom you come in contact.

Even though this experience was not a pleasant one, it gave me the opportunity to strengthen my character and learn that each obstacle placed before us strengthens to pushes us to greater responsibility. We are diamonds in the rough and must be shaped into beautiful gemstones. There is a solution to every problem; we just need to persevere until we find it. Each challenge brings us closer to where we want to be. It sharpens our mind and teaches what doesn't work. No two people are the same, but their experiences may be similar. You can empathize with, teach, and learn from others. I had six major turning points in my life. First when I was 19, I worked as a bookkeeper. I worked hard and it paid off, my employer paid me a large salary. I quickly advanced to manager. As fate would have it, my employer lost his fortune and I lost my job.

The second turning point was when I took a job as a sales manager. I knew nothing about sales, but I learned to take the initiative and find out what had to be done and do it before someone told me. I advanced rapidly again. I was highly paid and respected; I was on top of the world. I was greedy and vain. I thought money equaled success and the more money I had the more successful I was. Ah, fate awaited me again, like a stroke of lightning out of the sky. I lost my job and all my money. This was my first serious defeat. I mistook it for failure, but it was not it was only a temporary defeat. Every defeat teaches a lesson to those who are ready and willing to be taught.

The third turning point: I decided to leave sales and study law. I figured that if I was a lawyer I would gain back the money and respect I lost. I worked as a salesman during the day and went to law school at night. Along the way I realized the need for a school to train more salesmen, so I started one. It grew rapidly, and I expanded by borrowing money from a local businessman. This put me heavily in debt and I couldn't repay him, so he took over my business and once again and I was broke. I wandered to myself if there was something more of value then money and power at the end of my rainbow. It was a fleeting thought and I got a job as a lawyer and had money, power and respect again.

The fourth turning point: I resigned from my position at the law firm and moved to a different city. I worked at another law firm and worked my way up to partner. A friend suggested we go into business together and I agreed. Our business was extremely profitable. I was on the verge of finding my pot of gold. Then my partner and another associate wanted to force me out of the business without paying me. They had me arrested on false charges yet offered to withdraw the charges if I turned over my shares of the business. I felt like I had been stabbed in the heart with a dagger. I had lost my friends, money and business in one shot. I took them to trial for malicious damage to character and I had the chance to send them to jail until I had been paid back in full. I had a hard decision to make. I could take revenge, or I could show mercy and let them go. I choose the latter. Each temporary defeat left its mark on my heart. Each turning point brought me closer to the end of the rainbow and my pot of gold. It brought me useful knowledge, which became a permanent part of my philosophy of life.

The fifth turning point: The greatest way to learn is to teach others. So once again I started a school. It was successful for a few years and then students started going abroad to study and I was penniless. Unfortunate is the person who never had the thrill of being penniless at one time or another. Poverty is the richest experience that can come to a person. An experience which one needs to get away from as quickly as possible.

The sixth turning point: It may be obvious to you that I had not found my passion, my purpose in life. I could have remained defeated or I could pick myself up once again. Success is getting up after every fall. I sat down and started to write about my life experiences. The words flowed out onto the paper; little did I know that this was the foundation for the most important turning point of my life. That document I wrote not only influenced my own career but the lives of tens of thousands of men and women.

Defeat is a destructive force only when it is accepted as failure! When accepted as a lesson we need to learn it is a blessing.

I did not wish to return to prison, so I decided to take the old man's advice and forgive my former business partners. Three weeks after that conversation, my former partners were arrested and sent to prison for life. I got on with my life, rebuilding everything from the ground up. I got my family back and though life has its ups and downs its all worth it because we are all stronger and wiser. The blessing from this experience… Priceless

There is no failure for a person who has the perseverance to carry on.

Worksheet:

Know what you what and go get it.

When things seem to be going against you, it is your attitude that determines what the outcome will be.

There is no such word as failure for the man/woman who still fights on.
Be thankful for the defeat which some call failure, because if you can survive it and keep on trying, it gives you a chance to prove your ability to rise to great heights of achievement.
Life is a wheel turning from fortune to misfortune and round and round. In your greatest hours of trial and despair remember that "this too shall pass."
Every day is a new day, every minute you change the way you think about your situation. Press on, keep working and hoping for a better future. Be thankful for your problems and for the solutions you are forced to come up with.

The Thirteenth Key: Perverance

What are the problems you are facing today?

_____
_____
_____
_____
_____
_____

What are your choices?

_____
_____
_____
_____
_____
_____

What is your attitude?

_____
_____
_____
_____
_____
_____

What are your solutions? Your plan of action.

_____
_____
_____
_____
_____
_____

1. Close your mind to thoughts and people who are negative. Focus on the positive
2. Have a great desire to fulfill your purpose.
3. Make a plan of continuous action.
4. Find someone who can encourage you and help you reach your goals.
5. If your plan isn't working, change it and continue. Be persistent!

The Fourteenth Key

TOLERANCE

On the outside my clothes may be plain, so that I may mingle amongst the townsmen, but in my heart, I am born and bred nobility. After the war I joined friends on a journey to Canterbury. I wanted to relax before my next tournament. As I was leaving the Inn a man said he recognized me from a tournament in Greece. "Sir, you are a world-famous jouster, yet you treated the other competitors in Greece as though they were nothing. You are intolerant of people who believe in a different faith than you and are a different race or color than you." I was offended but he kept on talking. "Son, I want to share with you a key, this key is the fourteenth of fifteen and used together the keys will unlock your deepest dreams and greatest successes. They will turn your desires into reality. The only stipulation is that you must pass on the key to those with whom you come in contact.

As a warrior you fight along people of different cultures and religions, you join for the common cause of defending your country and give your life for each other. Then as soon as you take off your armor, you can't stand to look a Grecian in the eyes. Do you know that you are breeding contempt in your heart and that your children model their ways after you? The things we teach our children from the time they are born until the time they are 14 are instilled in their minds for the remainder of their lives.

Intolerance grows out of racial and religious differences of opinions as the result of early childhood training. Why do we try destroying one another because of their color of skin or different beliefs? Superficial matters over which we do not agree.

Our time on earth is but a fleeting moment. Like a candle we are lit, we shine for a moment and flicker out.

Why can we not live this short life in harmony with our fellow men?

When I die I hope to find only souls-Brothers and Sisters unmarked by race, creed, or color. I want to be done with intolerance, so that I may rest in peace not to be disturbed by the ignorance and petty misunderstandings that mark this world with chaos and grief. Study the facts; get to know people instead of judging them. Son, my purpose for giving you this key is to educate you and to awaken the power that

The Fourteenth Key: Perverance

lies sleeping within you. Develop the power and arise to action."

The conversation with the old man was unsettling to say the least. I am known around the world and have visited many different countries, was I intolerant of those people. It ate at me and I had many sleepless nights as I wrestled with that thought. If someone was willing to stand up to me and tell me the truth, maybe I should listen. It took some time for me to digest the criticism, but I wanted to teach my children to be the best they can, and that includes being tolerant of all mankind. I must lead by example and change the way I think and act.

Worksheet:

It takes a second to rebuke someone, but it takes them a lifetime to forget the one who rebuked them.

Memorize this pledge:
Promise yourself:
To be so strong that no one can interrupt your peace.
To talk health, wealth and happiness to everyone you meet.
To make all your friends feel valued
To look at life sunny side up
To think of the best, work with the best, be your best, expect the best.
To be just as enthusiastic about others success as you are your own.
To put your mistakes behind you and strive for great achievements in the future.
To smile
To give so much time to improving yourself that you have no time to criticize others.
To be too large for worry, too noble for anger, too strong for fear and very happy to cause trouble.
To think well of yourself and tell it to the world not in words but in your actions.
To get along with mankind.

The Fifteenth Key

FAITH

I love food, hunting, fine clothes and women. My vows of chastity and poverty as a monk are not written in stone. No one has ever been hurt by my actions. I still make my rounds to the poor, but the rich contribute more to my causes then any other monk. After confession, I went for a walk around the Canterbury Cathedral. A man approached me and asked me if I knew what the golden rule was? Embarrassed to say I did not know. "Son, I want to share with you a key, this key is the fourteenth of fifteen and used together the keys will unlock your deepest dreams and greatest successes. They will turn your desires into reality. The only stipulation is that you must pass on the key to those with whom you come in contact.

The Golden Rule means to do unto others as you would wish them to do unto you if the positions were reversed. The universal law that you reap what you sow. If you want great things for those around you, think great thoughts for them; wish them the best life has to offer.

It is not enough to believe in this philosophy you need to apply it in your relationships with others. If you want results you must take action.

If your actions are solely for accumulating wealth there is no warmth in your soul, no kindness in your words, you are too busy to enjoy life and too selfish to help others. You can never have success without happiness and no one can be happy without sharing happiness with others. Sharing happiness with others must be voluntary, without expecting something in return. You are spreading sunshine into the hearts of those who are heavy-laden with burdens."

I had not taken my vows to heart and used my position for my own personal gain. This man had made me realize faith is about treating others how I would like to be treated. My job as a human being is to give more than I take and to help others every chance I get. I have seen my weaknesses and am willing to change.

The Fifthteenth Key: Faith

Dear Reader,

When you have all 15 keys in your possession and use them together you will become an unstoppable force.

You must start with a purpose for your life you must live with *Passion*; you must have the *Confidence* to pursue that purpose; you must take the *Initiative* to use your confidence; you must use your *Imagination* in building the plans to transform your purpose into reality and putting that plan into action. You must mix in some *Enthusiasm* with your action. You must have the *Discipline* to take action each day. You must learn to go the extra mile and *Excel*. You need to build good *Character*. To have *Abundance* you must be responsible with the money you already have. You must have a *Vision* of what you are going to do and focus to get there. You must cultivate your relationships to produce good *Teamwork*. You must learn from your mistakes and have the *Perseverance* to try again. You must have *Tolerance* of those you encounter and those around you. Most important make *Faith* the foundation of all you do.

As a man thinketh in his heart, so is he. (Proverbs 23:7)

If thou canst believe, all things are possible to him that believeth. (Mark 9:23)

Faith without works is dead. (James 9:20)

What things you desire, when you pray, believe that you will receive them. (Mark 11:24)

Naked and you clothed me, I was sick, and you visited me, I was in prison and you came to me. (Matthew 25:31-35)

Ask and it shall be given you; seek and you shall find; knock and it will be opened to you. (Matthew 7:7)

Worksheet:

Read books to motivate you and share them with others.

How to read a book"
Step 1: Read the book all the way through, underlining important phrases, and writing notes in the margins. Do this with books you own.

Step 2: The second reading is to understand the details and new ideas.

Step 3: The third reading is to memorize phrases that apply to your life for future reference. Test new ideas use the ones that work and get rid of the ones that don't.

Step 4: When you get discouraged re-read your favorite books.

The human brain is like a battery and needs to be "recharged" by connecting with other more vital minds. Find a mentor in the area you are interested and learn from the best.

Also, a weekly "pep" meeting with talks by the leader or other speakers' "recharges" the mind and vitalizes everyone in attendance.

Stimulating the brain by brainstorming ideas in a group is also a good way to "recharge" your mind.

A "mastermind" group is usually a group of 6 or 7 people who meet regularly and are all working together to achieve the same goals.

Even when two or more people are concentrating on the same thing they can create a mastermind. You can achieve superhuman feats, power, and unlimited success.

FINALE

All fifteen went on with their lives. They made a commitment to share all they had learned with everyone they encountered. Years went by and one day the fifteen friends received news that the old man was dying, his last wish was to see them together he invited them all to his estate.

"Oh, it is so good to see you again. Have you each kept your promise?' He asked.
"Yes" they replied in unison.
"We have a gift for you" they told him "You have touched each one of us and made us better people, we in return have continued to teach others, come look out your window." They wheeled him to the window, outside was a sea of people. "These are just a few of the people we have taught and who have taught others."

"Thank you" The old man said meekly, a tear rolling down his cheek. "You have given me more joy then I could ever imagine."
They wheeled him back to bed; He never woke again.

.

Touching one life sends a ripple effect around the world

Take these keys, learn them, use them, and teach them and your ordinary life will become extraordinary.

www.ingramcontent.com/pod-product-compliance
Lightning Source LLC
Chambersburg PA
CBHW030903180526
45163CB00004B/1683